Published by Sheryl Spanier and Karen Otazo

ISBN 1442172428

www.sherylspanier.com

www.global-leadership-network.com

www.notime4theories.com

Author portraits: Ian Spanier
Editor: Nick Kolakowski
Graphic Designer: Mike Bain

Staying Power

Executive Fit and Flex

By Sheryl Spanier and Karen Otazo

Contents

INTRODUCTION: MAINTAINING CAREER STABILITY

"It is not the strongest of the species that survives, nor the most intelligent, but the one most responsive to change."

- CHARLES DARWIN

You see at least a few in every organization—executives who fly above the corporate storm clouds, emerge stronger from every restructuring and change, and gain support for their visions and initiatives from a wide range of coworkers both above and below them.

At times, it seems almost as if they possess some sort of magical stability and focus similar to the ability of troops in a location to stay solidly intact under duress, otherwise known as military staying power. You wonder, "How do they do it?" and you ask yourself, "How do I join their ranks"?

Staying Power: Executive Fit and Flex offers some strategies, tools and tips about being a leader who thrives through change and disruption, downturns, downsizings and mergers. This guide will focus beyond leadership competencies and resilience skills to include attitude, behavior and self-management techniques that will keep you aloft and in control, whether in churning or calm conditions.

It will enhance your ability to concentrate on those attitudes and behaviors that connect you with culture and people, rather than leave you rigidly following old patterns.

> If you want to:
> - Secure your foothold within an organization
> - Maintain your sensitivity and equilibrium during a transition
> - Rebound in the face of change and crisis
> - Use small triumphs to reduce the cycle time needed to adapt to new places or circumstances
>
> Then this guide is for you.

As a leader, you know that success and survival have become more difficult to assure. What worked before in the corporate world is not guaranteed to work now, and even best-in-class practices, your well-honed skills, style and long-standing supporters may not protect you from the bumpy ride ahead. You are being asked to adapt, shift priorities, find common ground with diverse and often contentious colleagues and find a way to rebound and portray equanimity in crisis.

Leaders who can bounce back—and assess, adapt and respond with grace to the constant barrage of bad news and disruption—will discover the opportunities in loss and reengage their own personal store of staying power. They free their energy to think and act in sync with their culture and conditions to make the right things happen— to Fit and Flex.

When you Fit and Flex, you play with all the reliable cards in your deck:

- Your characteristics (strengths, professional experience, style, values and preferences)
- Your organization's circumstances (the company life cycle and strategic stage, industry trends and challenges, and the economic and political environment)
- Your company culture (how things get done, the mores, the values and the subtle and unwritten rules)
- Your professional and personal connections (your stakeholders, sponsors, supporters, players and detractors, allies and adversaries)

The Vitality of Fit

Executives with staying power are often described as be-ing "a good fit" for their organizations. They quickly read the culture and work well within it. Such matches have little to do with luck when it comes to staying power.

As a talented executive, you Fit within your companies because you know how to integrate yourself seamlessly into the fabric of your workplace. You pick up on subtle cues from others about how best to work within the sys-tem—how to communicate, how to carry yourself and how to approach and include others. Leadership is situational, and you're sizing up the situation all the time.

Once you find the right equilibrium, you feel and ap-pear steady, no matter how rough the corporate skies be-come–and in return, you become a steadying force within your organization, keeping it on an even keel in the tumul-tuous and ever-shifting Post-Millennium business environment.

Culture Fit Is Powerful... and Subliminal

Fit is a finicky puzzle. In medium to large organizations, Fit can trump achievement at the executive level. Fit means you as an individual are congruent with the culture of the company and country in which you work.

"Culture," of course, is another puzzle to define. Countries have it; companies have it. It's a powerful force that helps define the individuals within, no matter who they are or what they do. For instance, when you go to China, you may notice that people getting into an elevator squeeze in much more tightly than Westerners would find comfortable. In global companies, headquarters often talk about needing a "comfort level" with local executives— that level of comfort is a must for all executives who move among corporate cultures.

Remember, staying power has to do with understanding and doing the right thing. It is about seeing which way the political winds are blowing and then going in the direction that matches the needs of the organization and the leader's vision.

The following profiles show how vital it is to mesh with your corporate culture while keeping your eyes on what matters. It can be a delicate balancing act.

> STAYING POWER IS ABOUT DOING THE RIGHT THING AND BEING AWARE OR THE ORGANIZATION'S CULTURE AND POLITICS, WHILE NOT BEING DRIVEN BY THEM.

DANGER SIGNS

"Mastering others is strength. Mastering yourself is true power."

- Tao Te Ching

The air is thin at 30,000 feet. The higher up you go, the harder it is to tell how you are actually perceived. High flyers are protected from critical Fit indicators that can make it or break it for them—nobody is going to tell the CEO that she has spinach in her teeth!

You Can't Fake Fit
Jill was president of a huge North American subsidiary, having risen in the ranks from engineer to unit leader, then division leader, and from there to the top. As a high achiever, she expected her colleagues and staff to do everything her way—and, given her drive and intelligence, she often did know best.

However, it was also her way or the highway. Anyone who wasn't a "Yes Ma'am" person lost his or her job. She loved subordinates who followed the rules and did as they were told. Although she led the American subsidiary, Jill had very few meetings concerning functions outside of her expertise; most conversations were handled over e-mail. When her team wanted to talk with her, it was difficult for them. Jill considered "face time" a waste of time.

Her team was afraid to have the slightest budget variance, saying "no" to any project that cost money—even though theirs was a capital-intensive business. When a local vendor suggested a viable idea to create a new income stream and needed startup money, her staff directed the vendor's team to a competitor rather than face her wrath.

As dissatisfaction spread across the U.S. company, key players started leaving disgruntled. Jill's cost-cutting measures hit a peak over the two years of her presidency, and she exulted in how much money she saved the company by not supporting any charities or community endeavors.

Yet, when the company's headquarters realized that the North American operations had stalled over a bit of cost savings, and the senator in the state in which they had closed a company facility called the company on the carpet, it was decided that a different leader should take over. Jill became the head of her specialty area worldwide and was replaced in her previous role by Jim. She later left the company.

RIGIDITY AND DRIVE
You can demonstrate a great deal of personal drive, and that will serve you well on your climb up the corporate ladder. However, your actions with others and your ability to stay in place and respond with your team, your boss and your peers make or break your organizational Flex and Fit.

You may come up through the ranks as technical or professional expert, and in times of stress you may revert back to your results-oriented way of doing things. You may do this at the expense of focusing on people, relationships and behaviors or style.

This is where the issue of Fit and Flex resides.

Early in your career, you advanced on the strength of your talents, achievements and results. Once a member of senior leadership, these actions and abilities are assumed, and your interactions and relationships (i.e., your management style and how you spend "face time" with stakeholders and supporters) gain more weight with regard to advancing your agenda. As you maintain the balance between a) what you do and b) how you do it, use this chart to check in with yourself; it will remind you to keep both elements in balance.

The Executive Path

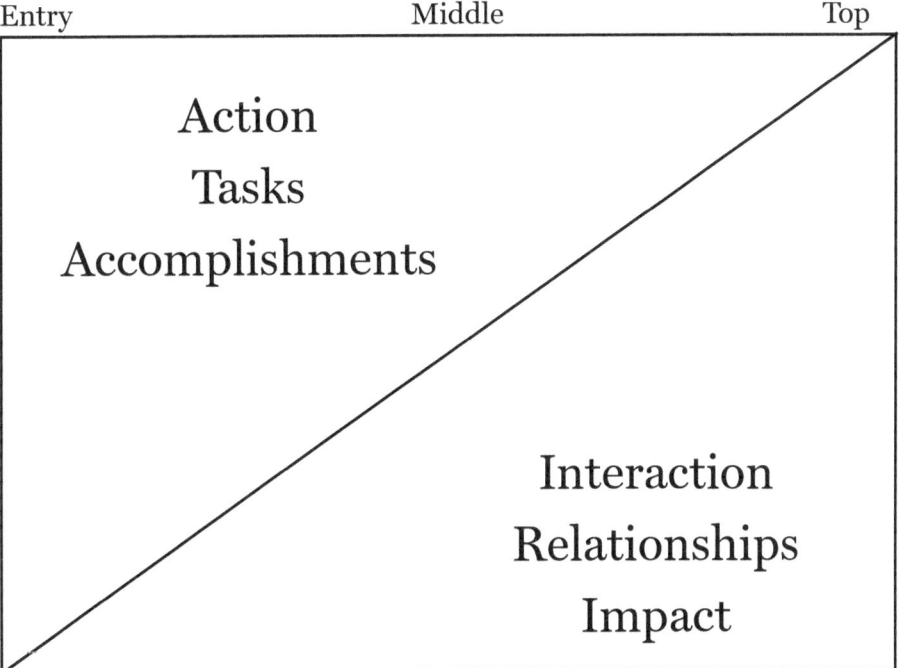

Entry   Middle   Top

Action
Tasks
Accomplishments

Interaction
Relationships
Impact

Stay the Course

You may have had a comfortable and secure Fit within your culture during your rise. But even at the top, you can lose ground and slip at either a professional crossroad or during organizational turmoil.

You might suddenly find your professional expertise and experience a poor match for the future of your business. For example, the advertising or media executive today needs to be nimble in the digital and virtual world, well beyond the traditional print environment in which he or she developed his or her successful strategies.

That being said, most leaders find themselves in trouble because of more ambiguous and interpersonal causes. Staying power demands that you be on the lookout for such "derailment factors." The Center for Creative Leadership uses this term to describe those minefields that appear in the path of previously successful executives.

* The center's research has shown that there are three major reasons for career derailment in the United States and Europe:

1. Inability to Develop or Adapt

Trouble in coming to grips with the way things are done in a new position or place of work.

2. Poor Working Relations

Failing to effectively network or build consensus with key stakeholders, or experiencing ongoing conflicts or communication problems with colleagues.

3. Organizational Isolation

Putting up boundaries around your unit or department, isolating it from the rest of the organization and from external influences.

[* See Appendix on page 55 for study information]

High fliers often go off course through a succession of behaviors or interactions about which they are completely unaware. Small rifts, missteps, inadvertent slights, power or people conflicts divert your position. You might never realize what is occurring until your path has been completely rerouted. The higher up you go in an organization, the less you know about how you are perceived and the impact of your behavior on reputation and results.

Top-level career killers:

- Deaf to feedback
- Drives results at others' detriment
- Misaligned with the boss/board
- Emphasizes speed over culture sensitivity
- Blames, shames, criticizes, complains
- Shows insecurities with dismissive attitude
- Cannot be trusted
- Aligns with the wrong people

Awareness Is Key
The most common reputation issues typically have their roots in communication and mood or emotion management.

When a lack of communication meets an inability to control your emotions or moods in a way that leaves the right impression, the rifts that open can be difficult to repair. Behavioral slips, as well as unintentional displays of negativity or insecurities, tend to manifest themselves when you're stressed, anxious or worried. Displaying nervousness in the face of uncertainty can be damaging.

How do you recognize if these derailment factors are present in your own career? Simply open your eyes, ears and mind. The people around you constantly send signals about your position and standing in the organization. Certain unintentional signals can often be revealing.

- Has your boss become less responsive to your communications?
- Do people work around you, not with you?
- Have you been left out of meetings or important projects?
- Do you get fewer invitations to lunch?
- Are you sought out for ideas, input or committees?
- How often are you involved in casual, friendly interchanges with respected colleagues and leaders?
- Are you among the first to know, or are you dependent on second- or third-hand "heads-up" comments?
- Are you sought out...or are you seeking after plum assignments?
- Are you an individual contributor or a team player?
- Do others welcome you into the room with eye contact and smiles?
- Are you appropriately copied on important e-mails, and are yours answered?
- When was your last career discussion or performance review? What was the main message?

Your answers to these questions will give insight into whether you are a valued member, or whether you are slipping out of the "core group" of people perceived to be essential to the organization. While excessive paranoia is to be avoided, being sensitive to others' signals may help you head off trouble early on. You may even be able to turn things around before those around you have become consciously aware of their own shift in their perception of you.

STEADYING YOUR COURSE

Executives with staying power are grounded in reality. They are able seek out feedback and take an objective look at their situation and work habits to determine whether they are well positioned or, alternately, need to reposition themselves or their organization when in a precarious spot. They keep their ears to the ground, their eyes open and their reactions in line with their goals.

So what can you do to get back on the right track?

Act Based on Feedback

- Solicit information and listen with true appreciation for the information...especially if you don't agree.
- Apply after-action reviews regularly. Reflect on what you decide to do, how you decided, analyze the outcomes, and make changes going forward.
- Take a hard look at your team's and your own behaviors and be honest about what may be working and not working.
- If necessary, ask a trusted advisor about what you may be missing, and be prepared to take that advice to heart and act on it.
- Consider and manage others' perceptions of your initiatives after first acknowledging where you are and where you need to be.

Take the example of a C-suite executive who realized that his combative/abrasive style was potentially putting him on the outs with the company. Even as he endeavored to try a kinder, more balanced approach to interacting with colleagues, the executive still found himself using the old way of coping with stress: abrasive language and shoot-from-the-hip reactions that put him at odds with others.

When this executive started reacting in the old way, he would say: "Please excuse me, I'm a recovering jerk." That way, the executive bought some time to change tactics; folks smiled and gave him a bit of leeway. He had learned the part he needed to play, and he played it more effectively by the day.

By altering how you speak to others, present your ideas and show your emotions, you can maintain an image of calm and restraint.

Be Tuned In
Jim came into the position as a leader who could galvanize employees. When he created and communicated his vision in conjunction with others, followers wanted to go where he led. Upon starting the position, Jim had an ambitious agenda (for example, he let his management know that he needed to start supporting countrywide investment in social programs and innovative projects to get the employees involved), but he knew that in order to enact it, he would have to build up credibility with the key members of his team. He needed to understand and do the right thing.

As the new leader, Jim immediately began building his organizational strength by connecting with all parts of the company, the community where the company was housed and the political leadership that regulated his industry. He treated everyone as a potential stakeholder, and he chatted with his CEO every other week. He even hung pictures of the company's workers doing their jobs on his executive floor, replacing the bland corporate art, and turned many of the offices there into meeting rooms for company employees, who now had increased access to him.

Jim knew that he didn't need to push for change in the company—just that he needed to become the role model for the company's culture. Once the employees believed in him, they wanted to follow where he led. He knew that his job was to convert employees, citizens and political leaders into stakeholders, and he sought to honor the informal norms in the company, which included connecting with bosses and asking questions.

To make sure that he was honoring the culture, Jim brought face time to a new level with company and community engagements—and whenever something important happened, good or bad, he sent out an e-mail newsletter letting folks know what was happening. As a constant and committed communicator, he spent his first year connecting all work locations within the company to create a dialogue about the new strategic vision; in addition, he used input from these sources to create a list of guidelines by which employees could know what really mattered in the company.

Great Fit	*Poor Fit*
Culture tuned in	Culture tuned out
Knows and supports what the boss wants	Ignores the boss
Gets input and takes action; perfect takes too long*	Expects perfect
Is appropriately open about what's happening	Keeps information secret
Hires smart people who question	Hires "yes" people who obey
Shows respect	Shows disrespect
Uses rules to create space for others	Uses rules to punish and control
Asks for whatever it takes	Punishes budget variances
Sets the vision and priorities	Focuses on hours and obedience
Models the way by giving others access to resources	Ties up company resources for own use

*Perfect is aspirational, not always actionable

Guidelines for Staying Power
Like Jim, you can assemble your own list of pointers to guide your Fit with your corporate culture:

GUIDELINE#1: GARNER AND GIVE YOUR BOSS SUPPORT

The person or group directly above you in the hierarchy has the most influence over your career. Think of your boss or your board as your first line of defense—and your greatest point of vulnerability. In a moment of transition, whether it is a reduction, promotion, or organizational shift, focus on the people who are in the best position to fight for your interests. Remember, all it may take is one negative word to torpedo your future.

How do you make sure that key players will go to the mat for you?

- Make them know you are critical to their success
- Make their lives easier
- Make them look good
- Keep them informed
- Customize communication to their preferred style
- Remember to show appreciation (even for small things)
- Recognize and respond to circumstance changes
- Monitor and manage your frustrations and reactions
- Manage bad news messaging
- Be visibly aligned
- Keep lines of communication open

You can ensure that there are no surprises, and that you clarify and confirm expectations, by taking charge of the focus, goals and agreements in any discussion with your boss/board.

Seven Clarity Drivers

Intentions: What do you want to achieve? What is your purpose?

Expectations: What do you expect will happen? What response do you anticipate?

Commitments: What are you willing to do, and what do you need your manager to do?

Deliverables: What is the end result of the negotiation? What will be the outcomes and benefits?

Deadlines: When is it expected?

Resources: What do you have/need to accomplish your goal?

Your Role: What specifically will you do to meet the mutual expectations? What will you need from your boss/others?

The Gift of Working It Out: Dialogue Worksheet

INSTRUCTIONS: Often, unresolved or unexplored miscommunications or gaps in style can expand to interfere with staying power. It is often your job to recognize and initiate the opportunity to talk. A dialogue is a gift for both of you. By initiating a conversation before a small misunderstanding becomes a big issue, you can establish mutual understanding and a plan to move forward together. See the opportunity to open up and talk together as a way of clearing the air and initiating the solution.

To benefit from the dialogue, plan carefully before conversing by considering the following:

GOAL: At the end of the meeting, what do you want to have happen?

INTENTION: What is the main message you wish to communicate?

FEEL: Are you comfortable with communicating clearly and objectively about the issues to be discussed? Come to terms with your feelings before you make the appointment or "pop in." Highly charged meetings generally are not as effective as those that are well thought out and considered.

TIME: Is there a sufficient schedule and appropriate setting for what you want to discuss? Choose a time and place that will make it possible to fully explore the issue and come to agreement or closure. Squeezing a conversation into an inappropriate time slot, when attention is not fully dedicated, when there is not enough time or where there is a lack of privacy will short-circuit your goals.

Also...

PACKAGING is critical to a win-win conversation. Present your ideas in an objective, thoughtful way and in a format that your manager prefers. He or she may prefer a top line written document, fully fleshed out "report" or a casual conversation. Analyze how you can present to your advantage and in alignment with your manager's preferences. If the conversation has a strong emotional component, think about the best way to create a business discussion, enabling open and interactive dialogue that is considered and measured while making the point.

GUIDELINE#2: BEWARE THE SMARTEST ONE IN THE ROOM SYNDROME

"Minds, like parachutes, only work when open."
                                        - THOMAS DEWAR

Do you find great satisfaction in pointing out errors, omissions and oversights in the interest of perfection? In negotiations, is being right your goal? Are you aware of the unintended consequences of your focus on irksome details that may not be vital to the outcome, or the impact of your reactions on others?

When you pounce on minutiae, you inspire a fear of making mistakes and stop others from setting their own priorities. You subject yourself to being the target of the blame-up process that labels you a "micromanager": a major leadership kiss of death.

Asserting yourself by indicating that everything you say is right and that you know the best and only way to go has several consequences.

- Others back off and hesitate to contradict
- Colleagues might use subterfuge or manipulate around you
- You appear arrogant and insensitive
- You lose the benefit of diverse ideas and input

No news is rarely good news for you. Most senior executives resist surprises. Yet, lack of information inevitably results in poor decisions, communication gaps, wasted energy and eventual derailment. So, do the opposite from your instincts and actively seek information before it goes underground.

A vehicle for making sure you encourage real-time evidence and information about how things are working is simply to conduct an informal or third-party data-gathering process, also known as "Managing by Walking Around" or "A Listening Tour."

Make this a habit as a normal process of business, before problems arise. When it is event driven, there is more suspicion, fear and secretiveness. The simplest way to proceed is to ask for feedback on your strategy, initiatives and progress on a frequent basis. You will get important data about the business and, not insignificantly, about your Fit and Flex.

	GOOD NEWS		BAD NEWS	
SURPRISE	**BUILD**	*Hidden Strengths*	*Blind Spots*	**REPAIR**
NO SURPRISE	**CELEBRATE**	*Conscious Strengths*	*Imbedded Flaws*	**FIX**

This model will help you sort through the information you receive and then plan for improvements. Process the results with a trusted advisor, mentor or consultant to assure objectivity and execution of a realistic plan.

The information you receive will be both familiar and surprising—and all of it will form the basis of your Fit and Flex plan.

A number of your actions, attributes and behaviors will be accepted as strengths; pay particular attention to these, as they give you valuable information about how you Fit and gain loyalty.

Some of these "strong" attributes may come as surprises to you; these are strong indicators of how you're valued.

You may gloss over the positive comments and observations. Don't. You can build solid staying power from a foundation of strength, rather than struggling to overcome weaknesses.

Pay attention to the "bad news" as well. Even though comments and observations may sting or seem unfair, these data are critical to your effectiveness and staying power. It is a gift to learn about others' opinions, particularly if a gap exists between what you intend and how others react.

Then, after you have processed and planned around the results, go back to your colleagues and share:

- What you learned
- What you will do
- How they can help

The trust and support you will garner is well worth the discomfort you may anticipate in the process. Given the chance, most people will want to be part of your success and will respect your desire to listen and grow.

Here is where Flex comes in—very often your greatest strengths are also areas that could afford a little extra attention on your part. For example, if you are gregarious and talkative, you may overuse these generally positive traits and be seen by others as dominating the conversation and not listening. Flexing this communication style to Fit with the needs of the situation and the sensitivities and styles of your audience will serve you well. The key here is calibrating your positive qualities to mesh with the circumstances.

A major complaint in exit interviews is that the senior management never seemed to listen. Even if you are the best listener in the world, if your staff believes the contrary to be true, then you have some work to do. Leaders lose great resources because they forget to ensure that others feel heard.

People cannot easily ignore a listening leader. In order to present your best "listening self" to others:

- Make eye contact; it shows that you are listening
- Show you are relaxed and open
- Use nuance to show you are hanging in there: nod, smile, affirm
- Indicate you care: remember and note small personal details
- Particularly when far away: stay connected with small notes, calls and e-mails
- Ban Blackberries during important conversations and meetings

People feel honored when they know someone has truly listened to them.

Look for chances to let your team know about positive experiences with them:

- When they've contributed significantly
- When they've met a goal
- When they've been supportive

Visiting personally is a powerful connection:

- Keep checklists about people you have touched
- Keep touches light and short
- Two-minute fly-bys can have more impact than long meetings

INFORMATION IS THE BEST WAY TO PAY:

In employee satisfaction polls, being "in the know" is often listed as being more valued than money. When we know what's happening, we feel included and involved.

Secrecy, on the other hand, breeds insecurity and in-fighting (just look at dysfunctional governments). It's your job as a leader to package information to keep your organization up to date whenever possible. A superb way to keep everyone informed is to have "skip-level" meetings to get to know the troops. In times of insecurity, this sort of touch creates additional stability while providing valuable information for you.

GUIDELINE #6: PUSHBACK IS A TRICKY ACT

When you invite pushback and then resist the results, you are putting others in a double bind. If they tell you what they truly think and are rejected, argued with or criticized, they learn quickly to tread softly.

Followers particularly appreciate leaders who ask questions and invite honest opinion and challenge. Complete obedience, on the other hand, breeds fear and a failure to try anything new.

Have an open energy and mindset and your staff will know you're open to their ideas. Ask questions, dispense praise when appropriate, and initiate brainstorming sessions in which "all ideas are on the table." Foster a spirit of creativity in the office; you can see the benefits for a company like Google when employees are encouraged to explore and activate their full potential.

WHEN SHIFT HAPPENS

"You never want a serious crisis to go to waste."

- RAHM EMANUEL

You could Fit one day and need to Flex the next. Without warning, the gears in your organization could become misaligned and stuck, and maintaining momentum will depend on your diplomacy and courage.

In order to best anticipate and roll with shifts, you'll want to check in with your staff, stakeholders and superiors frequently—particularly when you have an impulse to hide or run from tension and trouble.

A number of organizational events, often beyond your control and out of sight, exist as warning signs that your previously stable Fit needs Flex. During these challenges, your diplomatic and political skills, listening ability, stakeholder analysis and coalition initiatives are critical to your capacity to adjust to and align with sometimes radical and abrupt changes in style, culture and agenda. Some common examples are:

- New Boss or CEO
- Radical Change in Market Conditions
- Downsizing
- New Department or Team
- Change of Company Status
- Recovery
- Interim Assignment
- Relocation
- Overseas Assignment
- Promotion
- New Position

Build Collaborations and Connections

In the midst of a shakeup, culture change or political storm, you may find yourself aggressively putting numbers on a board to protect your organization and position. While in that headspace, you might operate without a keen regard for the critical people and context concerns that will lubricate change, growth and strength. You may reach the goal, but without engaging the political and cultural supports, there will be backlash, undermining and eventual talent exodus to deal with...or your own derailment to manage.

You can have the most laudable results and can even be a vehicle of much-needed change and still lose your staying power when you become focused on reaching the pinnacle of power through achieving the unachievable. The politics and the culture will get you every time!

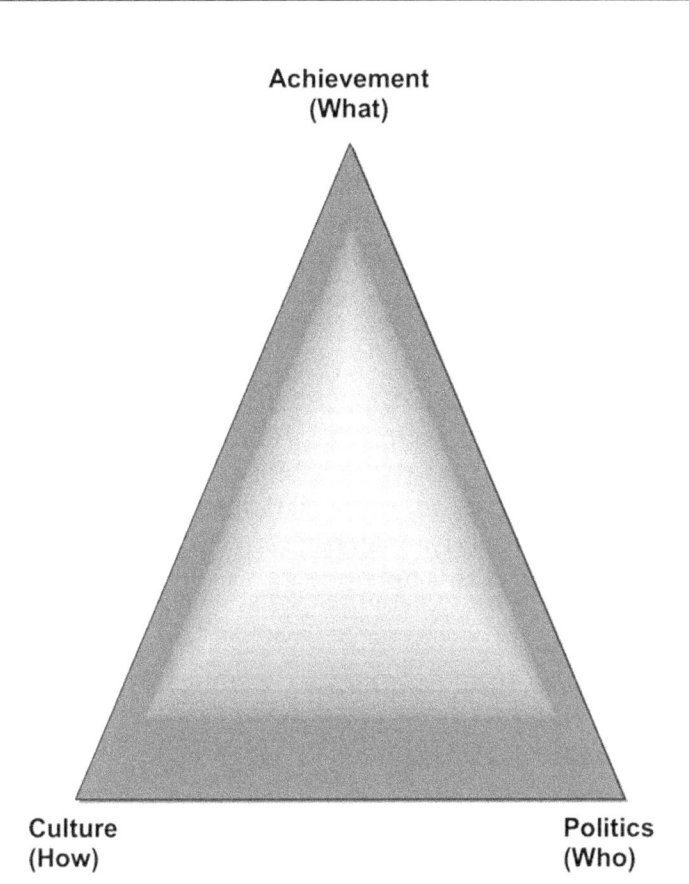

Achievement
(What)

Culture
(How)

Politics
(Who)

As this Achievement Triangle depicts, how you do something and whom you do it with and through are the foundations for getting things done.

The weight and impact of each element can change. Whatever matters most will shift with the goals and conditions in front of you. Remember, when you emphasize one, the others are modified.

Capitalize on Community

When you study great leaders, you find that those who crafted a sense of shared purpose and community built a solid set of supporters and coalitions and established a "comfort level" were the ones who produced lasting results. They had staying power. Lone Rangers who drive their agenda by numbers and rationale may get results, and can even occasionally be lauded for their brilliance, but without support and a following, they are unable to sustain their strategies when times get tough.

A critical component of staying power is your ability to construct and nurture supporters and stakeholders situation by situation. Your relationships with those immediately around you in your organization should form a fully illuminated and solid launch pad for your initiatives. Your vital connection points are:

- Your boss
- Your executive committee
- Your board
- Your boss's colleagues
- Your colleagues
- Your direct reports
- Your colleagues' direct reports
- Administrative professionals
- Groups that support you
- Organizational key executives and influencers
- Industry and professional key opinion leaders and connectors

Yes, building foundations to change, action or innovation is very time consuming. You might be pressured by your boss or board to be a change agent, to turn around a failing operation or to radically eliminate cost. You may have been recruited to do the "impossible." And these agendas are very seductive: after all, you can be the hero that saved the company.

> YOU MAY FIND YOURSELF THE TARGET OF CRITICISM FROM
> BOTH ABOVE AND BELOW IF YOU DO NOT CREATE A BASE OF
> OPERATIONS IN THE FORM OF BUY-IN.

Remember, all things being equal, you gain the greatest support by appealing to your stakeholders' and critics' enlightened self-interests.

Be patient while in the process of forming and attending to these important links. The swiftness of technology may make us think that all things can now be done quickly, but establishing trust and good feeling cannot be rushed.

You cannot "microwave" relationships; it is really a "slow-cooking" process.

These connections, stakeholders, sponsors and allies give you information and feedback and provide perspective. When you actively build, support and strengthen your foundation, you ensure your footing within the organization, as well as your visibility and connections in your industry or functional expertise. The broader your base, the more valuable you are.

STEP INTO YOUR ROLE

"A place on the stage is always better than a subscription in the orchestra."

- SCHOPENHAUER

Your organization wants to believe in you as a leader. Your job, with your management and your team, is to play your part well.

We can take leadership cues from Hollywood. The most effective actors talk about their bodies as "instruments" because they know that how they look, sound and move tells a story. In a similar way, you too are an actor—on the corporate stage. And like all great stars, your performance will be truly enduring when you remember to play to your audience.

Fortunately, many of the actor's tools that work on a soundstage also prove just as effective for a business-world performance.

Think of Martin Sheen or Meryl Streep, who have proven their skill over the years in a variety of challenging parts. Not willing to become typecast, they constantly reinvent themselves based on their maturity and audience appetites. They respect their writers, co-stars, cast and script. They are sensitive to meeting expectations with experience, listening carefully to reviews and applause. And should they (rarely) find themselves miscast, they reinvent themselves with the next part.

You are Always Auditioning
Your presence is under scrutiny, and it also has an immediate impact on results. Your reputation is only as good as your most recent performance with your "audience": your shareholders, staff and the media. As a visible, round-the-clock and global leader, you simply don't have the luxury to rehearse behind the curtain until you get it right—nor can you rest on your past performances; you will find yourself always auditioning, always on stage.

The imperative to play many roles as a senior executive can come suddenly. You may have been recruited and have thrived as a startup specialist, and now find yourself in a mature organization. You may be successfully heading up a turnaround and now have to lead an acquisition. Or your background as a technical expert/thought leader has carried you in good stead, and now you are being called upon to increase revenues with sales and schmooze. Often, the stretch requires re-jiggering your well-honed skills.

IN THE GROOVE

Think of how challenging it is for a classically trained opera singer to perform a jazz song. The technical musicality may be there, but getting in the groove could very well result in an awkward adaptation that just falls flat for the audience. As an executive, you may also have found yourself in situations where you are required to adapt your expertise and experience into a new rhythm.

In the end, it is all about the audience: As you and your organization go through various trends and demands, you may find yourself improvising and re-calibrating your well-honed expertise in courageous steps, based on a quick read of the audience. The best strategy, unless well executed, dies like a bad joke or dropped line. Your ability to carry the message, be convincing and confident is a play-by-play event.

Showtime

When you step onto your leadership stage, remember your role based on your current goal. If your focus is on driving courageous change, your posture, tone, script and intention can elicit a shared vision and understanding of what it will take to work together toward the goal.

Regardless of your personal doubts or concerns, your role is to drive commitment, optimism and accountability. Presidents Abraham Lincoln, Franklin Roosevelt and John Kennedy were expert performers in tough times, leading their constituencies and detractors alike to believe and transform their own roles to support their leader's inspiring worldview.

Leaders are performers who inspire their audience through a variety of roles:

Coach
Mentor
Psychologist
Motivator
Executor
Strategist
Salesman
Presenter
Listener
Visionary
Producer
Politician
Diplomat
Entrepreneur
Innovator
Key thought leader
Catalyst

Your Stage Presence
As you take the leadership stage, consider your presence. What impression, reaction, impact or action do you want your performance to create?

Chita Rivera is a wonderful example of "presence" as it applies to Staying Power. As a young woman, she took on Broadway in the lead role of *West Side Story*. As she matured and tastes changed, she adapted into many roles in many productions, including *Kiss of the Spider Woman* and *Bye Bye Birdie*.

At the age of 70-plus, Chita found herself starring in *Nine* with the much younger, charismatic performer Antonio Banderas. Onstage during one of his more dynamic songs, this veteran performer got the audience's attention not by upstaging him, but by quietly, calmly and assertively entering stage left, making eye contact with the audience and waiting until all eyes were on her before uttering a word or making a motion. With a few simple and artful mannerisms, she commanded everyone's attention; this truly was stage presence.

> "PRESENCE" IS A SOLID AND ENGAGING DEMEANOR THAT NEITHER COMPETES NOR UPSTAGES, YET DRAWS FOLLOWSHIP FROM THOSE SURROUNDING YOU.

Commanding Tone

Think of the classic "leader" sound. Generals and principals have it, and everyone who hears it knows who's in charge. A combination of short, precise sentences, spoken without hesitation and delivered in a low-pitched but clearly audible voice with a stop at the end of phrases and sentences solidifies an in-control and assured leadership impression.

Long sentences can sound unsure, tentative and weak. And tone and pitch make a big difference. At the end of a sentence, moving your voice down, rather than up in a questioning style, displays confidence. A rising tone tends to imply uncertainty or a request for permission. Visualize ending your sentences with a declarative exclamation point.

In order to generate your "gravitas" tone:

- Move the source of the sound from your throat to your ribs
- Breathe from your abdomen and relax your neck muscles
- Make your throat and mouth your instrument, like a trumpet or horn
- Keep your body relaxed
- Imagine air between your words

Space

You send powerful signals to others about your position in the hierarchy by the way you enter, position yourself and walk. When you act as if everyone needs to make way for you, you reinforce that you are in charge. Take up space in a room with intentional mannerisms, using your arms and hands in strong, sweeping motions that extend out from your shoulders.

Think about your entrances and exits. Onstage, the use of silences, spaces and anticipation all give the script extra "oomph." It's not about keeping people waiting—just about making clear that you have control and gravitas. People need to see you as dependable and competent while also understanding implicitly that they can't take advantage of you to make unreasonable demands.

Script

Use strong language when you want to evoke strong reactions. You waste your power when you speak strongly all the time. Avoid strongly positive and negative terms, especially when dealing with challenges, toxic events, difficult decisions and tough people issues.

Utilizing emotionally neutral terms and mannerisms lowers the chance of receiving negative reactions. Be careful about what words you use, as strong emotions of any kind can provoke defensive behavior in others. They may feel that you are trying to push or dominate them, and they may react abrasively in return.

When using emotionally laden language, consider what effect you are trying to create in your audience. It's not that you shouldn't let people know whether you are happy or unhappy—you simply need to be selective about when and how you do that. Keep what you're thinking private until there is an appropriate moment to raise it, and then do so in a neutral and considered way. Thus, you appear focused and in control. Your words have more impact when not wrapped in the "noise" of emotion.

Many a stage actor has recovered from a flubbed line or a dropped cue by inserting a bit of humor or a wink to the audience. In the same way, should your actions lead to a mistake, a bit of humor and a lot of honesty on your part can help endear you to any observers.

Make Your Performance Stick
You have more than a reputation: You have a story. Everyone does. People love narrative so much that they can't help telling stories. We tell stories about each other and, often without realizing it, we tell our own story.

So what's the word on the street about you? In every place you work, you will have a story, and it will affect how the people you work with perceive you and whether they want to follow you. You may know part of it but rarely all, as some things will never be said to your face. Such information, however, can be a true tipping point with regard to your staying power.

Your story spreads each time someone talks about you at work and when others repeat parts of what they hear. Once a certain story takes hold, it can be hard to shake off. Get angry about something in a meeting once early on, for example, and you may be labeled an "emotional" person for the foreseeable future.

THE POWER OF PRODUCTIVE POLITICS

"You can have anything you want in life, but you do have to pay attention. What you don't pay for with attention, you pay with pain."

- ANCIENT HAWAIIAN SAYING

You've heard it over and over again:

"It's all politics!"

"That person is so political!"

"I don't like playing politics."

"Politics" has a pejorative tone, as if working the crowd and selling your plans are somehow demeaning and unseemly. The word has a nasty reputation, mainly because of the nastiness of government politics. Nasty politics impedes progress and creates actions and retributions that can block progress and momentum. People accuse others of having an "agenda" or Machiavellian intentions.

Staying Power is all about working the politics: An understanding of and ability to unearth and coordinate with the agenda, needs, goals, issues and self-interest of both powerful and powerless people around you. To ignore politics is like saying, "It's only germs" during an influenza epidemic.

Used wisely and with generosity, politics can be a productive and supportive aspect of your endeavors.

Ignore politics at your own peril

Anytime you get more than two people together, you will have politics. Naïveté about politics shows ignorance and professional immaturity.

Politics allows you to stay in power as a leader. Whether or not you want to play in the political realm, you have to be constantly looking at who is in power, whose ring you need to kiss and with whom you need to cozy up in order to get something done.

Executives with staying power know that getting things done and staying on top are all about politics. They get others to buy into their agenda, vision, initiative or change. Flexible, politically astute leaders can switch-hit between commanding, selling and educating their constituencies. They stay attuned to the external pressures and realities and get best results by understanding the range and limits they have in their world.

You may resist the idea of working the political landscape, particularly if you have observed destructive politics in action by inept players. Political spoilers are not always obvious in their actions, but they twist the situation to suit their aims. They can undermine with faint praise, directly wound with a well-placed criticism or create barriers to forward momentum by passive-aggressive behavior...or outright obstruction.

Conversely, political "maximizers" understand how to build coalitions by building on enlightened self-interest and honoring the needs and values of their constituents. They can get support by talking with key players and stakeholders before endeavoring to accomplish anything.

Inoculate Yourself Against Viral Politics
The key to protecting yourself against toxic politics is to be skeptical and keep your mouth shut until you have formulated a strategy:

- *Quid Pro Quo*: A "You support me, so I will support you" approach can create loyalty.

- *Covering*: Help your best buddy look good.

- *Watch Your Back*: Be aware of snakes, but never confront them directly.

- *Undermine the Underminers*: Do this cautiously, however.

- *Beware Story Triangles*: This is when rumors and innuendo are spread about someone to a powerful source or, in conflict-averse, indirect cultures, when people speak about others to third parties rather than directly.

How do you diagnose and inoculate yourself from destructive politics? Act like a scientist and hypothesize. Test others with something very small to see how they handle it and where the information goes.

- Will someone keep secret a negative opinion, or speak supportively and positively about others?
- Do people talk directly with each other...or about each other behind their backs?
- If you share an innovative idea with a colleague, will he help you succeed, or adopt and promote that idea as his own?
- If you write a confidential e-mail, will it be forwarded to others?
- Will your boss or board fully back you up when you are placed in a tenuous or risky spot?
- What do your colleagues say to you about other people? Do you sometimes feel like you are in junior high school?
- How active is the rumor mill?

PAY ATTENTION TO POLITICS...
BUT DON'T LET IT DRIVE YOU

Seven Stealth Political Moves

1. Identify your collaborators
2. Contain your competitors
3. Manage up
4. Coach and develop down
5. Communicate and collaborate across
6. Build coalitions
7. Use Nemawashi *

---

* See Appendix, page 55

Likeability in Leaders

Since 1960, Gallup polls conducted prior to every U.S. presidential election have shown that of three personality factors polled—issues, party affiliation and likeability—only one has consistently predicted the winner: likeability.

People vote for and buy from, marry, want to work with and spend time with people they like. When people like you, life and work get a whole lot easier.

So what makes you likeable? You don't have to be the life of the party. In fact, you should aim to be more like a host or diplomat, focused on making others feel at home. By easing transitions, anticipating needs and filling them in a smooth manner, likeable people make life easier for everyone around them.

When you're a leader, likeable means being someone on whom others can depend: A "broad-shouldered" chief who extends an air of gravitas. Being viewed in such a way can greatly help build a support foundation for your goals and initiatives.

Likeable leaders do the following:

- Elicit trust
- Trust others 360° (boss, peers and direct reports)
- Proportion their ask/tell ratio
- Give direct and clear feedback
- Praise and encourage
- Honor confidences
- Act with respect
- Set and confirm realistic expectations and clear deliverables
- Deliver on promises
- Show empathy above judgment
- Utilize a sense of humor

When people like you and enjoy being with you, they lower their defenses and become willing to invest more in your agenda. By doing so, they strengthen your visibility and support. These contacts, stakeholders, sponsors and allies give you information and feedback and provide perspective. They can guide you and create a smooth path by connecting you with others, and you can reciprocate. This way, you foster and expand your support system.

You will want to constantly maintain your contact infrastructure, particularly in steady times and well before you hit rough terrain that could threaten you with derailment.

BROAD-SHOULDERED LEADERSHIP

In these times of stress, transition and shaky economies, your team needs your calm, assertive and unshakable self more than ever. Promote your staying power by creating a set of guidelines for yourself and your staff:

1. Stay calm and consistent, even during times of stress, frustration or anger; your mood is contagious.
2. Get out of your office and get a feel "on the ground."
3. Calm employees down when they're worried or anxious.
4. Create limits and boundaries at work; ensure that the employees understand the rules and the rationale for honoring them.
5. Provide information, which is as important as compensation.
6. Put important messages in writing; keep them short.

Face Time and the Grapevine
The Irish call it the "craic." On Wall Street, it's the "squawk." Everywhere else, people most likely call it the "grapevine." Whether at the water cooler or online, it's what every executive needs to both stay in the know and make sure that others are in the know. Whatever you call it, it's that give-and-take information conduit that's so vital to executive success and staying power.

Once plugged into the grapevine, you can test your thinking to get reactions and can stay abreast of developments in a surprise-free way. Those looking to test, question or filter can even add information into it.

When participating in the grapevine, however, filters are necessary:

1. Act "dumb" and think dirty
Keep your mouth shut, and question the motives behind any information you receive. You only know for sure about the veracity of news and ideas you hear when they are tested.

2. Test veracity
Run ideas or information you have past others to help determine truthfulness and viability.

3. Double check with those you trust
They may put down ideas that others hold up as gospel— or vice versa.

4. Entice engagement
One easy way to access the grapevine is to draw others toward you. Back when he served as a major in the Air Force, one executive kept a huge jar of chocolate candy on his desk. He never had trouble getting face time with his superiors, colleagues and staff because they would always stop by to raid the jar. By using the time they spent in his office to ask questions, he got a sense of what was happening on the base and how he could best fit in.

Consider setting out your own personal "chocolate jar" and seeing how a few minutes' visit by others can help boost the information flowing to you.

When inserting information into the grapevine, take a page from those political candidates who "stay on message":

- *The news flash*
  Make sure you impart information in a concise way. An excellent model for this is the "news flash," a 30-second brief that is supposed to concisely and compellingly "give an update."

- *Keep it upbeat*
  In any communications situation, a positive and informational message will set people at ease and convince them to open up in turn.

- *Keep the gossip to a minimum*
  Remember, it's all about idea generation, expanding options and showing what you can offer, as opposed to dishing the latest dirt.

- *Watch out for assumptions, prejudgments and blind spots*
  These can harm your message and prevent you from anticipating situations.

- *Shape your story*
  Be aware of how your story will play "on the street," and tailor accordingly; imagine how the information will sound after it's been conveyed by two or three people down the chain of communication.

When you connect regularly with enough and varied sources, you are not only in the know, but can also manage what they know.

STRATEGIES FOR STAYING AFLOAT

The Physical Side

Faced with a tense team, business failure or a conflict-ridden organization, you will no doubt have a physical reaction. You may lose sleep or experience muscle tension, headaches or digestive reactions. You may find yourself off-kilter or feeling exhausted, and you might even catch colds or the flu more frequently. These symptoms are early warning signs that your staying power might be at risk.

Pay attention to these physical signs early, and you will redirect yourself away from a potential "doom loop" of feeling weakened, slower responses, poor results and increased physical symptoms.

Applied early, there are many ways to keep calm and controlled in the face of such stressors. Harness your own energy to shape your team's reactions and support the culture you built. Here are a few techniques:

Recognize and reduce tension

- Become aware of your own body reactions to tension. All strong reactions start with tight muscles.
- Examine the myth that the only way to relax anxiety or anger and work off tension is through hard, sweaty workouts—many people also do well with calmer physical arts, such as meditation, tai chi or yoga.

Take three deep breaths

- Sit still in a comfortable place.
- Inhale through your nose.
- Concentrate on breathing into your diaphragm. If you place a hand on your stomach while inhaling, you will feel a "push."
- Breathe in for a count of three and hold the breath for a one-count. Then, exhale slowly, counting to three.
- Repeat three times.

Calm your mind

- Learn basic mediation. Press a finger against one nostril. This will decrease the amount of air reaching your lungs and make you take slower, deeper breaths—making you slow down.
- Listen to music or sing along with a favorite song. Music, particularly singing, has been shown to relax the brain.
- Close your eyes and picture a beautiful scene. This will refocus your attention and provide much-needed relief.

Change your body posture

- If you are leaning forward, lean back in your chair.
- If you are holding onto something, such as the arms of a chair, let go and put your arms in your lap.
- If your arms are folded, unfold them.
- If your head is thrust forward, align your head with your back.
- If you are standing, sit down.

The Cerebral Side

Staying power is also a mind game; following certain rules of engagement when having conversations with others will make such interactions run far more smoothly. At the same time, keeping a bit of perspective on your situation will also help.

Use descriptions rather than assessments

- Use neutral words when describing situations.
- Avoid labels like "stupid" or "dumb."
- Before using a harsh word, stop and correct yourself: Instead of saying, "That's a career-limiting move," try something like, "You might consider asking for feedback before taking action."
- Give an alternative behavior when you see something that's not working.

Wait for others to finish speaking before you respond

- A response any faster than that may seem abrupt.
- A moment of silence is better than stepping on others' points.

Think ahead

- Set your intentions before all interpersonal engagements; think about what you want to happen, and you won't have to push for it.
- Keep positive. Prayer, meditation and taking a moment to "see the big picture" will help.

Know When to Hold... And When to Fold
No matter how well you Fit or how astute you are in reading and Flexing with the corporate culture, you may assess that the juice is no longer worth the squeeze. Either the organization or you could change. It is critical that you recognize this early so you can preserve your well being, career identity, reputation and legacy. You may want to consider whether it's time to explore other options and move on.

Staying Power is also about knowing when it is time to Leave Happy. * Ironically, you may be staying at the table too long in support of the desire or need for job security. This can sometimes work against the interests of both you and an organization, especially if you could be happier and more effective somewhere else. Sometimes you need to know when to hold, and when to fold.

It is often smart to retain your career staying power, reputation and integrity by making a change before your career is derailed or your organization suffers. Little can be gained by trying to bend yourself into a pretzel simply to stay in a position that isn't working for you or anybody else.

* Please refer to our guide by this title

So, sometimes staying power is really about leaving. But before you run for the door:

Make a list

- Objective observations
- Subjective rationale and interpretations
- Support systems
- What you have done about the issues
- What you could do
- What you want to do

Consider all options

- Unexplored internal opportunities
- Relationships to build or fix
- Actions to ameliorate the situation
- Change of perspective
- Bridges to rebuild

Seek advice

- Confirm your conclusions and explore alternative ideas
- Talk with people you trust
- Meet with external mentors and advisors
- Encourage them to ask you hard questions

Recognize the opportunity in challenge

- Might this be a development opportunity?
- Can you learn something new?
- Can you leverage this experience later?

Remember your relationships

- How you leave is how you will be remembered
- Position yourself in your exit statement
- Keep relationships intact
- Don't complain, blame or attack

CONCLUSION: YOUR PATH TO STAYING POWER

"Take the first step in faith. You don't have to see the whole staircase. Just take the first step."
                        - MARTIN LUTHER KING, JR.

It is a daunting task, and maybe not what you signed on for. Beyond making sure your short- and long-term strategies are being executed, you must ensure on a daily basis your resilience and creativity in your constantly changing market and workplace.

You will parachute into a variety of cultures and, once on the ground, you need to show sensitivity to myriad business and communication mores. You will need to assess and adapt to marketplace and people crises both unexpected and awesome. As conditions change, you can apply your experience and perspective to assess and adapt. Knowing when to hold fast, change course or vacate in a storm will be the predominant leadership effectiveness tool in tomorrow's world of work.

As a leader, you will be more of a diplomat than a director. The key is to quickly get the lay of the land and then walk through it with grace and gravitas. You will constantly be called upon to transverse the intersection where your actions and organizational demands intersect. Becoming adept at recalibrating how to Flex in the diverse ways that will get things done with (and through) others is something that becomes a habit through practice.

You can be expansive and engaging, building your political and cultural foundations for action. Use the varied tools at your disposal to build your staying power. Just as a diplomat never steps onto foreign soil without a careful analysis of the local players and culture, so you too can tune into your ever-shifting (and perhaps restructured) corporate culture and figure out how to mesh with it. Demonstrating Fit, and then Flexing to Fit in, will be the key to your Staying Power.

> LEADERS WITH STAYING POWER ARE A "TRIPLE THREAT":
>
> - THEY READ AND RESPOND TO SIGNS AROUND THEM.
> - THEY ADAPT.
> - THEY BUILD AND ADD SHARED SUCCESSES.

APPENDIX

* The study on page 14 is "Why Executives Derail: Perspectives Across Time and Cultures," by Ellen Van Velsor and Jean Brittain (1995), published in the Vol. 9, No. 4 Journal of the Academy of Management Executive (now the Academy of Management Perspectives).

* Nemawashi, referred to on page 44, is an informal process of quietly laying the foundation for any proposed idea, change, project or initiative so you talk with everyone privately before public meetings.

Dr. Karen Otazo has been a global executive coach and mentor for executives in transnational companies worldwide for more than 25 years. Her second book, The Truth About Being a Leader (2007), was recognized as one of the Top Five Best Business Books for 2007 by Strategy and Business.

Dr. Otazo's experience makes her uniquely equipped to work with executives connecting cultures in global corporations, national subsidiaries, international ventures and strategic alliances.

She sits on the boards of Vital Voices Global Partnership, Citizens for Affordable Energy and Best Partners. Karen is a fellow of SoL, the Society for Organizational Learning, an international learning community dedicated to sustainable business.

www.global-leadership-network.com

Sheryl Spanier is a thought leader, media contributor and master practitioner of Executive Career Management who is sought out to coach and advise international leaders and their teams. After working as a consultant and market leader for four premier career management companies, she started her own firm in 2004. With more than 25 years in the field, Spanier combines empathy and pragmatism to coach clients in maximizing the interpersonal side of their business strategies and to lead individual and organizational change.

She is a member of Phi Beta Kappa, a founding member of the Association for Career Professionals International and is certified as a Fellow by the Institute for Career Certification International.

www.sherylspanier.com

www.ingramcontent.com/pod-product-compliance
Lightning Source LLC
Chambersburg PA
CBHW051246170526
45165CB00004B/1598